HOW THE US GOVERNMENT WORKS

HOW THE JUDICIAL BRANCH WORKS

by Christine Petersen

Content Consultant
Luke Bierman
Dean and Professor of Law
Elon University School of Law

Core Library
An Imprint of Abdo Publishing
www.abdopublishing.com

www.abdopublishing.com

Published by Abdo Publishing, a division of ABDO, PO Box 398166, Minneapolis, Minnesota 55439.

Printed in the United States of America, North Mankato, Minnesota
092014
012015

Cover Photo: Orhan Cam/Shutterstock Images
Interior Photos: Orhan Cam/Shutterstock Images, 1; AP Images, 4, 16, 21; Fuse/Thinkstock, 7, 24; Photos.com/Thinkstock, 9; Shutterstock Images, 11, 32; iStockphoto, 12; North Wind Picture Archives, 14; Library of Congress, 19, 39; Bettmann/Corbis, 22; Red Line Editorial, 26, 28; Charles V. Tines/The Detroit News/AP Images, 30; Pablo Martinez Monsivais/AP Images, 34, 45; Evan Golub/Demotix/Corbis, 40

Editor: Lauren Coss
Series Designer: Becky Daum

Library of Congress Control Number: 2014944232

Cataloging-in-Publication Data
Petersen, Christine.
How the judicial branch works / Christine Petersen.
p. cm. -- (How the US government works)
ISBN 978-1-62403-636-1 (lib. bdg.)
Includes bibliographical references and index.
1. Courts--United States--Juvenile literature. 2. Procedure (Law)--United States--Juvenile literature. 3. Law--United States--Juvenile literature. 4. United States--Politics and government--Juvenile literature. I. Title.
347--dc23

2014944232

CONTENTS

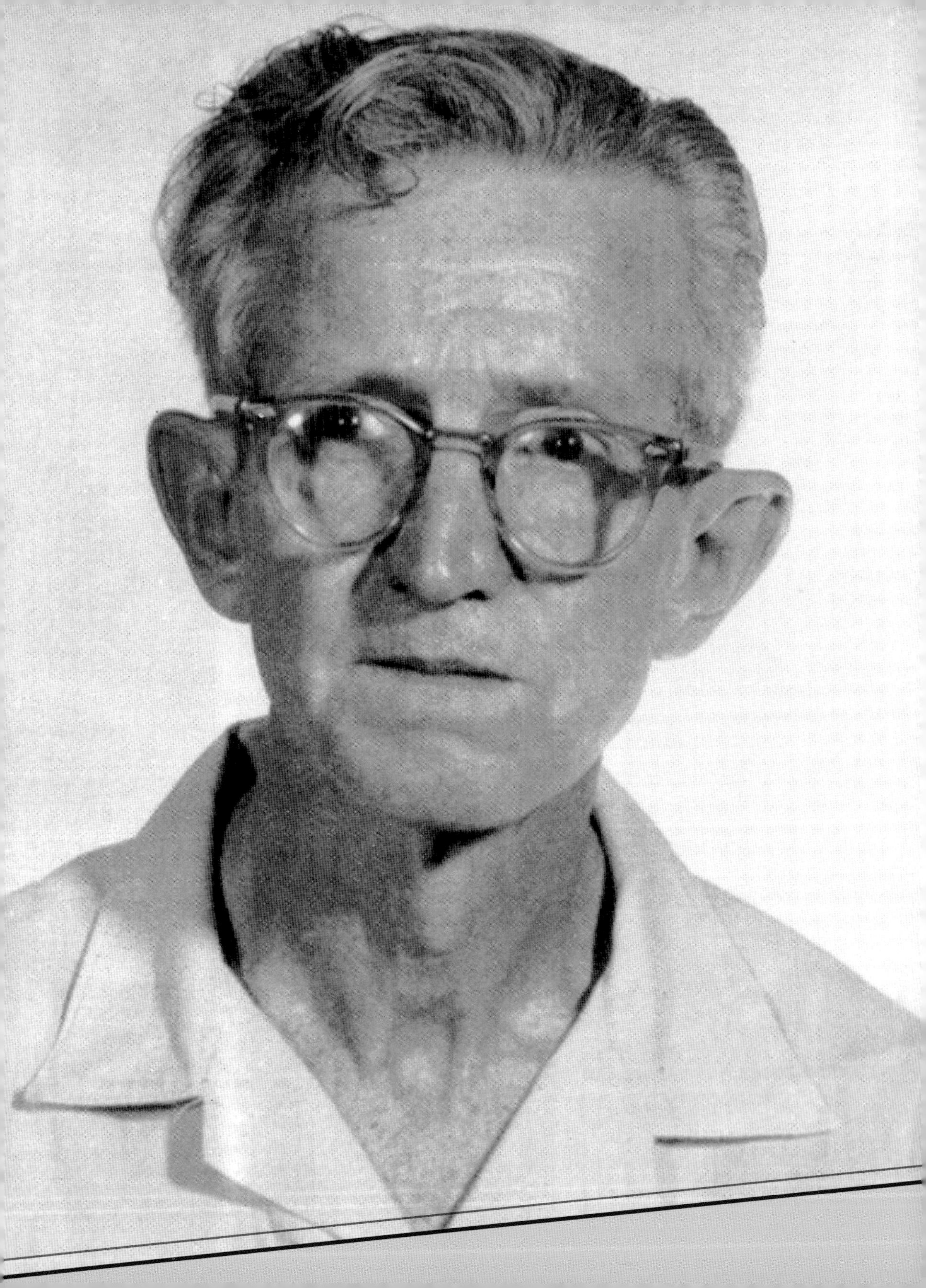

CHAPTER ONE

Seeking Justice

In 1961 Clarence Gideon stood before a judge in Florida. The 51-year-old man had been accused of breaking into a local business and stealing money from its vending machines. A witness claimed to have seen Clarence Gideon at the scene of the crime. Gideon insisted he was innocent. But he could not afford to pay a lawyer. He asked that one be provided to him. The judge refused. Gideon

Clarence Gideon's appeal to the Supreme Court helped change the law so all people accused of crimes were able to have lawyers, regardless of their ability to pay for one.

had to speak for himself during the trial. He was convicted of the crime and sentenced to five years in prison.

Gideon Appeals

While in prison, Gideon studied US law. The Sixth Amendment to the US Constitution says that everyone must be allowed a lawyer to defend them in federal court cases. Gideon believed he should have been allowed a lawyer.

Gideon asked that his case be heard by Florida's highest court. He was turned down. But Gideon

The Sixth Amendment

Ten amendments, or changes, were added to the US Constitution in 1791. Together they are known as the Bill of Rights. The amendments describe freedoms shared by all Americans. The Sixth Amendment calls for the right to a fair and speedy trial. It also mentions that all US citizens are entitled to a lawyer. Before Gideon, some courts had interpreted this to mean that a lawyer could be banned from representing an accused person. They believed the court only needed to provide lawyers for very serious crimes, such as murders.

The Supreme Court building in Washington, DC

kept appealing. In 1962 the Supreme Court of the United States agreed to review his case. A lawyer represented Gideon free of charge. In 1963 Gideon and his lawyer stood before the nine Supreme Court justices in Washington, DC. Gideon's lawyer explained that Gideon had been too poor to hire a lawyer for his first case. Because Gideon was not allowed one, his conviction was unconstitutional.

The justices listened to Gideon's argument. Then they talked together about his case. All nine justices said that Clarence Gideon had been denied his basic rights as an American. In the future, courts would make sure the state or federal government provided a lawyer to anyone charged with a crime who couldn't afford a lawyer. Gideon was freed.

The Judicial System's Beginnings

The US Supreme Court, Florida's highest court, and the original lower court where Gideon was denied a lawyer are all part of the US judicial system. This is the system of all the courts in the United States. The US judicial system has it roots in England more than 800 years ago. At that time, England's King John was demanding huge taxes from people in his kingdom. Those who did not pay were punished. The king took their land and property. People formed an army to fight back against the king and his taxes. The army demanded that King John either step down as ruler or agree to treat the people more fairly.

In 1215 King John signed the Magna Carta, a document that gave the English people greater power in the government.

In 1215 the king signed a document called the Magna Carta. It promised that a trial must take place before the government took any free man's land or property as punishment. Both sides had to be heard. A jury of other free men would decide whether the punishment was fair. In time, juries were used in many other kinds of trials.

America declared independence from Great Britain in 1776. Early American leaders believed the Magna Carta laid out a good system. In 1788 they approved the US Constitution. This document

Checks and Balances

The authors of the Constitution worried that someday a leader or branch might try to take over the government. So each branch was given ways to check, or limit, the others' power. For example, the legislative branch must approve people appointed to office by the president. The president may veto, or reject, a law passed by the legislative branch. And the Supreme Court can decide that a law is unconstitutional. This way the power of the federal government is balanced among its three branches.

The Three Branches of Federal Government

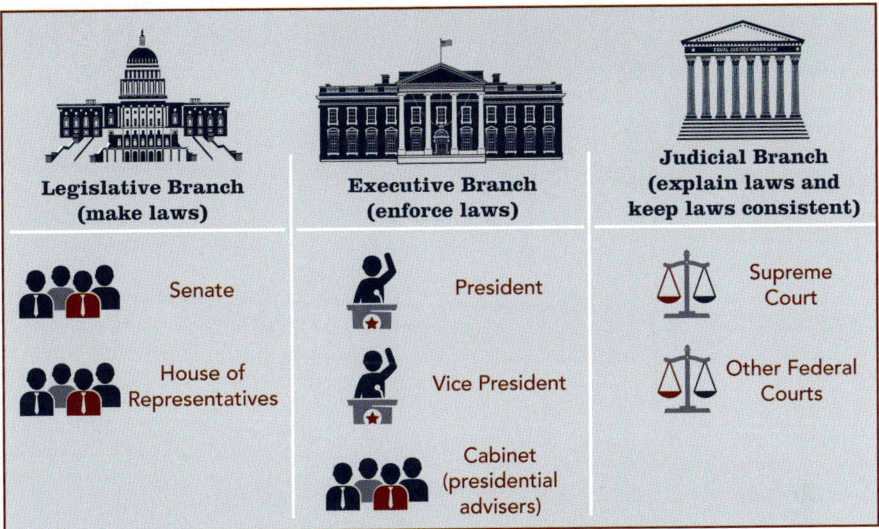

This diagram shows the three branches of the federal government and the responsibilities of each. Does it match what you understand about them? How does the graphic help you better understand our federal government? What questions does it raise?

explained how the new nation's government would work. There would be no king or monarchy. The United States would be a republic. The people would elect their own leaders.

The new nation's government included three branches, or sections. These branches would be independent of one another, but they would work together. The legislative branch was known as

As the first US president, George Washington was the head of the young nation's executive branch.

Congress. The people elected to Congress would make the nation's laws. Led by the president, the executive branch would enforce laws. The third branch of government was the judicial, or court, system. It would be responsible for explaining laws, making sure they were consistent with the Constitution, and using them fairly to decide cases. The American judicial system does its best to make sure that laws are used the same way in all cases.

STRAIGHT TO THE SOURCE

In 1931 nine African-American boys in Alabama were accused of attacking two white girls on a train. Eight of the young men were sentenced to death after a one-day trial. However, Supreme Court Justice George Sutherland explained why this was a violation of the boys' rights:

Even the intelligent and educated layman has small and sometimes no skill in the science of law. . . . He is unfamiliar with the rules of evidence. Left without the aid of counsel, he may be put on trial without a proper charge, and convicted upon incompetent evidence, or evidence irrelevant to the issue or otherwise inadmissible. He lacks both the skill and knowledge adequately to prepare his defense, even though he [has] a perfect one. He requires the guiding hand of counsel at every step in the proceedings against him. Without it, though he be not guilty, he faces the danger of conviction because he does not know how to establish his innocence.

Source: Powell v. Alabama. 287 US 45. Supreme Court of the US. 1932. Louisiana Public Defender Board. LPDB.LA.GOV, n.d. Web. Accessed July 16, 2014.

Consider Your Audience

Identify the main idea in this passage. Consider how you would explain this information to a different audience, such as a younger sibling. Write a blog post explaining this main idea to your new audience.

CHAPTER TWO

The Court System Begins

The Constitution formed our federal government and created the Supreme Court. But it did not describe the judicial system in detail. Lawmakers were left to decide how many courts were needed and how the courts would be used.

The first Congress under the Constitution met in 1789. The new nation was divided into 13 districts.

President George Washington was key in developing the Constitution and the early judicial system.

John Jay was the United States' first Chief Justice. Later he became governor of New York.

Its legislators decided to set up circuit, or local, courts in each of the districts. Three similar courts would meet the needs of Americans living in the countryside. Each of these lower courts had one judge. The Supreme Court would oversee the lower courts. The Supreme Court was assigned six justices. President George Washington chose New York political leader John Jay to be Chief Justice. He would lead the other five justices. As the nation grew, so did its court system. Beginning in 1807, more justices were added. Today nine justices are on the Supreme Court.

The Court's First Case

The original justices of the Supreme Court held their first session in New York City in February 1790. The law required the court to hear cases twice a year. But there were no cases for the court to hear until August 1791. The first Supreme Court Case was *West v. Barnes*. Mr. West of Rhode Island had borrowed money to buy land. He wanted to pay off the loan using Rhode Island's paper currency. Mr. Barnes was a

Riding Circuit

For 121 years, Supreme Court justices also heard cases in the federal circuit courts. Every justice was responsible for three circuit courts. He traveled to them twice a year to hear cases. This became known as "riding circuit" because the justices rode on horseback or in horse-drawn stagecoaches. In the mid-1800s, justices began riding trains instead. But traveling to circuit courts still used up huge amounts of time, energy, and money. As the number of cases increased, the government finally made a change to the system. After 1891, Supreme Court justices no longer had to travel to hear cases in circuit courts.

lawyer. He spoke for the family from which West had borrowed. He insisted that West had to pay in gold or silver.

The justices saw that West had a reasonable case. Yet they ruled in favor of Barnes. West had to give up the land. The law says that a person must follow certain steps before the Supreme Court will hear their case. At that time, a person had to have paperwork signed by the court's office in Philadelphia, Pennsylvania. But West lived far out in the

An illustration from 1883 shows the Supreme Court justices being flooded with cases.

country. He went to a circuit court in Rhode Island instead. But that court was not authorized to sign for the Supreme Court. Barnes won because he had followed the right procedure.

West v. Barnes became an important case. The justices realized the law was unfair since rural people could not easily reach the right courts. They asked President Washington and Congress to change the law. Rural people could now register Supreme Court cases with their local courts. They didn't need to travel to faraway cities to register their cases.

Segregation

When the Constitution was written in 1787, slavery was legal in the United States. The Thirteenth Amendment banned slavery in 1865. And in 1868, the Fourteenth Amendment to the Constitution said that states must give all Americans "equal protection of the laws." That meant states could not legally prevent African Americans from entering public places. But especially in the South, some states insisted that the races remain segregated, or apart. The areas set aside for African Americans were much worse than those for whites. African Americans faced horrible racism and discrimination. Their schools had poorer supplies, which meant the students often didn't get as good an education.

The Supreme Court worked to make sure laws served all people. In 1800, it moved to the nation's capital, Washington, DC.

Landmark Cases

Life today is very different from when the Constitution was first written. The Constitution's authors designed the document so it could change and grow over time. New federal laws were written and adapted to meet Americans' new problems and needs. But these laws have to follow the Constitution. The Supreme Court

Only 60 years ago, many businesses still had signs indicating that African Americans were not allowed inside.

plays an important role in deciding which laws need to be rewritten to make them consistent with the Constitution and fair to Americans. The Constitution has also been challenged many times. Sometimes it needs to be amended.

Supreme Court cases that play a role in changing a law or laws are known as landmark cases. One of the most important landmark cases came before the court in 1952. The case was known as *Brown v. Board of Education*. In it a group of African Americans sued several Kansas school districts because they required black and white children to attend different schools.

Lawyers George Hays, *left*, Thurgood Marshall, *center*, and James Nabrit, Jr., *right*, celebrate in front of the Supreme Court building after winning *Brown v. Board of Education* in 1954.

Brown was part of a group of four similar cases the court heard at the same time. The court originally heard the case in 1952, but it couldn't come to a decision. It heard the case again in 1954.

This time the Supreme Court justices all ruled that separate schools were unequal and harmful to children of color. States would be required to let children attend school together.

STRAIGHT TO THE SOURCE

In 1954 Chief Justice Earl Warren wrote the Supreme Court's opinion, or the written statement of the court's ruling, in *Brown v. Board of Education*. He said:

> *Today, education is perhaps the most important function of state and local governments. . . . It is required in the performance of our most basic public responsibilities, even service in the armed forces. It is the very foundation of good citizenship. Today it is a principal instrument in awakening the child to cultural values, in preparing him for later professional training, and in helping him to adjust normally to his environment. In these days, it is doubtful that any child may reasonably be expected to succeed in life if he is denied the opportunity of an education. Such an opportunity, where the state has undertaken to provide it, is a right which must be made available to all on equal terms.*

Brown v. Board of Education. 347 US 483. Supreme Court of the US. 1954. Legal Information Institute. *Cornell University Law School, n.d. Web. Accessed April 22, 2014.*

What's the Big Idea?

Take a close look at this text. Use a dictionary or ask an adult to help you look up any words you don't know. What is Warren's main point about education? Pick out two details he uses to make this point.

On Trial

The judicial branch of government is divided into state and federal systems. State courts handle state law cases. These include most of the cases in which a person is accused of a crime. People and businesses also use the state courts when they need help to solve disagreements. These are called civil cases. Special state courts are set up to help with adoption, divorce, and other family matters.

A prosecuting lawyer may question a witness during a trial, trying to prove the accused person is guilty.

State and Federal Court Systems

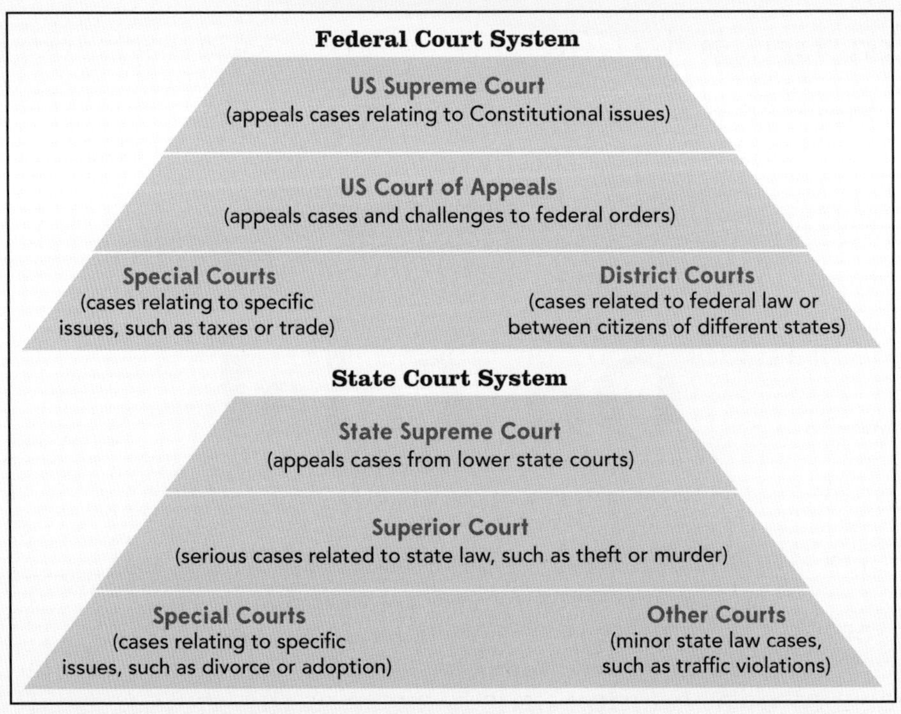

The state court system has three levels. The federal system also has three levels. This diagram shows different levels of state and federal courts. How does the information presented compare to what you read in the text?

State judges are selected in many ways. They may be elected by voters or chosen by the governor. Others are selected using a combination of these methods.

Federal courts have a different focus. They usually hear cases about federal laws, arguments between states and residents of different states, and questions about the US Constitution and what it allows. The president of the United States chooses federal judges, who must then be approved by the Senate.

Inside a Criminal Trial

In state criminal trials, the accused person is taken before a judge soon after being arrested. The suspect's lawyer is present for this meeting. The prosecutor, or the lawyer who will conduct the case against the suspect, is also at the meeting. The police officers who arrested the suspect must also attend. A judge usually explains the charge, or reason for the arrest. Then the suspect and his or her lawyer respond.

The accused person, known as the defendant, may choose to plead guilty. Then the judge decides a sentence. That may involve jail time or a payment of money, called a fine. If people have committed a less serious crime or were never arrested before, the judge may give them a light sentence. It might include community service or paying a fine.

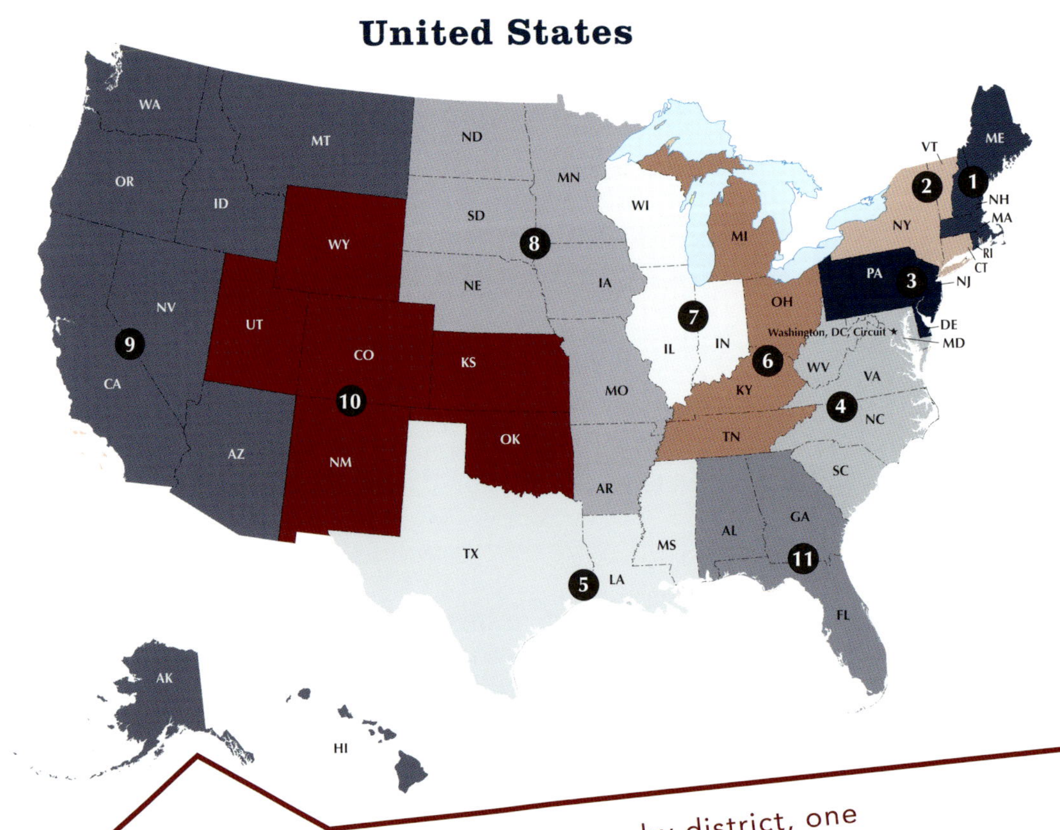

Eleven circuits serve multiple states by district, one serves Washington, DC, and the thirteenth is the federal circuit.

People are sometimes accused of crimes they did not commit. Others refuse to admit to doing wrong. These suspects can enter a plea of not guilty. Others plead *nolo contendere*. This means they will not plead guilt or innocence. Once in a while, a lawyer claims that a defendant is guilty by reason of insanity. In other words, the person was not clear-minded when the crime took place. Therefore the person should not be held completely responsible. After any of these pleas, police continue their investigation of the crime. They search for evidence. Meanwhile the suspect may be held in jail or released on bail. That means the suspect pays the court to be temporarily released. The court returns the money if the suspect comes back to court when expected.

At the Hearing

The next step is a hearing. A judge listens to the lawyers present. Then the judge decides if the evidence is strong enough

Traditions

Police and lawyers use the latest technology to investigate and present their cases. Judges and justices have access to a huge online library to help with their research. Yet the courts are also quite traditional. This is especially true of the US Supreme Court. Justices have worn black robes for more than 200 years. Lawyers are expected to dress in formal suits when presenting a case. And the court always has a supply of feather-quill pens at hand, just like those used by the first justices.

During a hearing, the judge will decide if there is enough evidence to put the accused on trial.

to go forward in a trial. If so, a date is set for the official trial.

The US Constitution says a defendant must be considered innocent until proven guilty. The prosecutor tries to present evidence that shows guilt. He or she may bring in witnesses who know something about the crime. They may show an object or document that connects the person to the crime. The defendant's lawyer may present evidence that shows the defendant did not commit the crime.

Some cases are only heard by a judge. In other cases, the defendant may ask for a trial by jury. A jury is usually made up of 12 adults chosen from the community. The jury looks closely at all the evidence presented by both sides. Its members must all come to an agreement about the suspect's guilt or innocence. The jury then gives a verdict, or decision. The judge chooses a sentence when necessary.

Serving on a Jury

Juries have been around for a long time. The oldest record of trials by jury dates back about 2,400 years. In ancient Greece, any male citizen could call for a trial. Other men might choose to serve on a jury. There were no judges, so the jury decided the case. US juries are made up of adult citizens from the local community. Jury duty is an important part of citizenship. Participating on a jury gives Americans an inside look at the judicial system. As jurors, citizens can help uphold laws and protect the rights we all share.

Appealing a Verdict

In both state and federal trials, the defendant may appeal a verdict. This means he or she submits a

People serving on a jury will listen carefully to both sides of a case.

request for an appeals court to review the original court's decision. Each state has many trial courts and fewer appeals courts. Most states have only one supreme court, which also hears appeals. The federal court system also has fewer appeals courts than trial courts.

Defendants must have a good reason to appeal a decision. The defendant must prove the original court made a mistake during the original trial. An appeals court's decision is usually the final decision on cases. If it's a state case, the only way it can be overturned is if a state supreme court hears the case. Federal cases can be overturned if the defendant presents the case to the US Supreme Court or another appeals court.

EXPLORE ONLINE

The website below has even more information about state and federal courts. As you know, every source is different. Reread Chapter Three of this book. What are the similarities between Chapter Three and the information you found on the website? Are there any differences? How do the two sources present information differently?

Comparing State and Federal Courts

www.mycorelibrary.com/judicial-branch

CHAPTER FOUR

Court Is in Session

Each year on the first Monday of October, the nine justices gather to begin a new session of the Supreme Court. The nation's highest court meets in a marble-columned building just a block from the nation's capitol in Washington, DC. People attending court walk along the wide Great Hall to enter the large Court Chamber.

This photo of the nine Supreme Court justices was taken shortly after Elena Kagan, top right, was appointed to the court in 2010.

Justices take their seats on a high bench in the front of the courtroom. Court workers sit below, to the left and right. They help keep the court organized and on time. Wooden tables in front of the bench are for lawyers and their clients. When it is his or her turn to speak, each lawyer steps up to a platform facing the justices. Behind a railing, special seats are available for reporters and visitors. Visitors are permitted while the court is in session.

Justice for Teens

Many cases have had a direct impact on children and teens. In 1943 the court determined that students are not required to salute the American flag at school. In 1987 the court decided that students did not have a right to use offensive language in speeches in school. A 2000 court decision banned students from reciting prayers at public school events. Like adults, teens must be given due process when they are in trouble. This means that young people must be told about the steps that will be taken during discipline and have the chance to appeal.

The Court's Cases

About 10,000 cases are filed every year for the Supreme Court to consider. Each case is carefully reviewed. The justices pass over some cases because they agree with the verdict that has already been delivered by a lower court. They mainly accept cases that can impact how we use and understand federal laws. The modern Supreme Court usually agrees to hear no more than 80 cases a year. Both sides in a case have a chance to write up and submit a document explaining their side of the story. The two sides then exchange those papers, and each writes a shorter reply to the other's comments.

Once a case has been accepted, it is added to the court docket, or calendar. The justices hear cases on Monday, Tuesday, and Wednesday mornings from October through April.

During this time, the two sides of each case appear in court. The Supreme Court is very formal. Each session begins when the marshal of the court calls out, "Oyez! Oyez! Oyez!" This means, "Hear ye!" in the Anglo-Norman language, a dialect spoken in the 1100s in England. It is a reminder to be quiet in court. Everyone stands when the justices enter. The lawyers have no more than 30 minutes to present their cases.

Later the justices discuss the cases they have heard. Each justice gets a turn to speak, beginning with the Chief Justice and ending with the justice who was most recently appointed. The justices listen to one another. Then they vote. The majority of votes decides the

A Diverse Court

On October 2, 1967, the Supreme Court welcomed a new justice. Thurgood Marshall became the first African American to sit on the court. In 1916 Louis D. Brandeis became the first Jewish justice. In 1981 Sandra Day O'Connor broke a different barrier. She was the first female justice. Sonia Sotomayor is one of the most recent justices. She was appointed to the Supreme Court in 2009. She is the first Hispanic justice. Today the Supreme Court represents the diversity of our nation more than ever before.

Thurgood Marshall served on the Supreme Court from 1967 to 1991 as the first African-American justice.

case. One of the justices writes an opinion that summarizes the court's decision. Other justices may write a reply that explains the opposite point of view. The justices deliver all opinions before the court ends its term on June 30 each year.

Becoming a Justice

Supreme Court seats do not often become open. The nine justices hold office for life or until they choose to retire. On those rare occasions, the president chooses a candidate. The Senate must interview that

A crowd outside the US Supreme Court building on June 26, 2013, waited to hear the Court's ruling on the Defense of Marriage Act.

person. It then has the right to reject the president's choice. There are no requirements for age or level of education to become a Supreme Court justice. Candidates do not even need to be lawyers. But they must show a deep understanding of and respect for the law.

Justice for All

The US Supreme Court has heard hundreds of cases over the years. It has made decisions that affect all of us in many ways. In 2013 the Supreme Court ruled against the Defense of Marriage Act, a law that banned same-sex couples from receiving the same legal benefits as other couples. The court's ruling paved the way for many states to legalize same-sex marriage.

The judicial system is not perfect. But for more than 200 years, it has worked to serve Americans. By learning about the rights and responsibilities of citizenship, we can all work for justice.

FURTHER EVIDENCE

Chapter Four looks at the Supreme Court and its cases. What was one of the chapter's main points? List one or two pieces of key evidence that support this point. Visit the website below to learn more about the Supreme Court. Does the information on this website support the main point of the chapter? Does it make a new point? Write a few sentences using new information from the site to support the chapter's main point.

Frequently Asked Questions About the Supreme Court

www.mycorelibrary.com/judicial-branch

IMPORTANT DATES

1215

England's King John signs the Magna Carta, stating that all free men are entitled to a trial by a jury.

1788

The US Constitution is ratified, or passed, establishing the new nation's system of government.

1790

The US Supreme Court opens its first session, held in New York City.

1954

The Supreme Court case *Brown v. Board of Education* determines that it is unequal and illegal to put children in separate schools based on race.

1963

The Court hears *Gideon v. Wainwright* and declares that criminal defendants must be provided a lawyer if they cannot afford one.

1967

Thurgood Marshall becomes the first African-American Supreme Court justice.

1791

The first ten amendments, known as the Bill of Rights, are added to the US Constitution.

1800

The Supreme Court moves to Washington, DC.

1891

Supreme Court justices no longer have to travel to circuit courts.

1981

Sandra Day O'Connor becomes the first woman to serve on the Supreme Court.

2009

Sonia Sotomayor is appointed to the Supreme Court as the first Hispanic justice.

2013

The Supreme Court rules against a law preventing married same-sex couples from receiving the same legal benefits as couples of opposite sex.

STOP AND THINK

Why Do I Care?

The Constitution set up our judicial system more than 200 years ago. That doesn't mean it is unimportant to modern life. How does the judicial system affect your life today? Think of some of the landmark Supreme Court cases discussed in this book. What might your life be like if the court had ruled differently? Use your imagination!

Tell the Tale

Chapter One of this book discusses the trial of Clarence Gideon. Write 200 words that tell the story of Gideon's trial and appeal. Describe his experiences and the way he might have felt in court. What might he have been worried about? Be sure to set the scene, develop a sequence of events, and offer a conclusion.

Surprise Me

Chapter Three discusses differences between federal and state courts. After reading this book, what two or three facts about these courts did you find most surprising? Write a few sentences about each fact. Why did you find them surprising?

Dig Deeper

After reading this book, what questions do you still have about the judicial system? Write down one or two questions that can guide you in doing research. Ask an adult to help you find a few reliable print or Internet resources. Write a few sentences to summarize what you learned.

GLOSSARY

appeal
to ask that a case be judged again in hopes of a different decision

appoint
to choose a person to do a particular job

bail
money paid by a person accused of a crime, allowing them to remain out of jail until trial

convict
to declare a person is guilty of a crime

defendant
the person being sued or accused of breaking the law in a court case

evidence
proof that something happened

justice
a judge in a court of law

majority
more than half

monarchy
a government ruled by a king or queen

plea
a response to charges in a court case

prosecutor
the lawyer who presents a case in court against a defendant

verdict
the judge or jury's decision in a case

LEARN MORE

Books

Britton, Tamara. *The United States Supreme Court.* Minneapolis, MN: ABDO, 2004.

Schmidt, Maegan. *The US Constitution and Bill of Rights.* Edina, MN: ABDO, 2013.

Websites

To learn more about How the US Government Works, visit **booklinks.abdopublishing.com**. These links are routinely monitored and updated to provide the most current information available.

Visit **www.mycorelibrary.com** for free additional tools for teachers and students.

INDEX

ABOUT THE AUTHOR

Before becoming a freelance writer, Christine Petersen enjoyed diverse careers as a bat biologist and middle school teacher. She has published more than 60 books for young people, covering topics in science, social studies, and health.